BUILT TO FATHER

The Study Guide

For the Man, the Marriage, and the Men Around Him

Doug Androsky

Author of Built to Father

"Be watchful, stand firm in the faith, act like men, be strong. Let all that you do be done in love."

— 1 Corinthians 16:13-14

Published by Douglas Androsky
ISBN 979-8-9955281-5-9
First Edition
SHEPHERD Framework™, Built to Father™, and Fathering the Fatherless™ are trademarks of Douglas Androsky. All rights reserved.
Printed in the United States of America

Built to Father: The Study Guide is part of the *Built to Father* Series.

Built to Father Series

Book One
Built to Father
The SHEPHERD Framework for Fathers

Book Two
When the Framework Fractures
The Complete Diagnostic Companion to Built to Father

Book Three
Built to Father: The Study Guide
13 Sessions for the Man, the Marriage, and the Men Around Him

This book is the application workbook for *Built to Father*. It is designed to be used alongside that volume — not in place of it.

Built to Father introduces the SHEPHERD framework: eight interconnected pillars of fatherhood that define what it means to father with intention. This Study Guide moves through all eight pillars across 13 structured sessions — built for three contexts: a man working through it alone, a husband and wife working through it together, or a small group with a facilitator guide and a weekly accountability commitment that every man names and is held to.

If you are also carrying fractures in specific pillars — areas where you can see the cost but are not yet sure what is broken — the second book in this series, *When the Framework Fractures*, maps all 247 failure combinations across the SHEPHERD framework. It is a diagnostic companion, not a reading book. Use it to locate your specific situation. Use this guide to do something about it.

Most men do not fail at fatherhood because they do not care. They fail because no one ever showed them what it looks like. This guide is for the man who is done with that excuse.

Built to Father and When the Framework Fractures are available wherever books are sold.

TABLE OF CONTENTS

How to Use This Guide

Built to Father argues that God designed fatherhood intentionally — and that most men are operating on default, shaped more by the fathers they had (or didn't have) than by the Father they were made to reflect. The book builds a framework called SHEPHERD: eight pillars of biblical fatherhood, each one a dimension of what it means to be the man your family needs. This guide takes that framework and turns it into practice. It is designed to move you from reading to doing, from knowing to becoming.

This guide is not a summary of *Built to Father*. It is an instrument for applying it. There is a significant difference between a man who reads a book and a man who lets a book do something to him. This guide is for the second kind of man.

It can be used in three ways.

SOLO: Work through each chapter section on your own after reading the corresponding chapter. The individual reflection questions are designed to be answered in writing, not skimmed. The write lines are there for a reason. Use them. A man who writes his answers is a man who cannot avoid them.

WITH YOUR WIFE: Several questions in this guide are designed to be answered together. Chapters 4 (Husband Who Loves Sacrificially), 12 (When You Have Failed), and 13 (Rise) are particularly well-suited for couples who want to do this work together. These are marked with a note. Do not skip the hard questions. Those are the ones that matter.

WITH A SMALL GROUP: The group discussion format in each session is built around a 55-minute meeting. The facilitator guide that follows this section contains everything a group leader needs to run the sessions well. Read the facilitator guide before your first meeting. All of it.

> *Note for men in different situations: this guide is written for four kinds of men — the present father with a gap, the absent father looking for a way back, the fatherless man about to become a father, and the man who had a great father and wants to pass it forward. Most questions will fit all four. Some will not. If you are estranged from your children, translate the questions about "your children" into "the children you are trying to return to" — the question is still yours. If you do not yet have children, translate them into "the child you are about to have" — the answer is still worth writing. The questions are not tests of your situation. They are invitations to the work.*

> *Note on honesty: Every question in this guide has a version of the answer that sounds good and a version that is true. The version that sounds good will not change anything. The version that is true is the one worth writing down.*

Your answers in this guide are yours. No one else needs to see them unless you choose to share. But if you are doing this in a group, the most important thing you can bring to every session is the truth of where you actually are — not a polished version of it.

The Group Covenant

A covenant is not a set of rules. It is an agreement between men about who they are going to be to each other for the duration of this journey. Sign it. Mean it. Return to it when the group drifts.

We will be present.
We will show up. We will silence our phones. We will be here — not partially, not on the way to somewhere else, but actually here with the men in this room.

We will be honest.
We will not perform. We will not give the answer that sounds good when the answer that is true is different. We will say what is actually happening in our homes and in our lives.

We will hold the line for each other.
When a man in this group makes an accountability commitment, we will ask him about it the following week. Not to shame him. To remind him that his growth matters to us.

We will keep what is said here.
What is shared in this room stays in this room. A man who cannot trust the confidentiality of the group will not bring the things that matter most. We protect each other's honesty.

We will not fix each other.
We are not here to solve each other's problems. We are here to be present to each other and to ask the questions that help a man find his own answers. The Holy Spirit does not need our assistance.

We will pray for each other.

By name. For each other's wives and children. For the specific struggles each man carries. The group that prays together is building something that outlasts the thirteen weeks.

We will finish what we start.

We will complete this guide together. If a man is struggling to stay in the group, we will reach out before we assume he is gone.

Signatures

Name	Date	Name	Date
Name	Date	Name	Date
Name	Date	Name	Date
Name	Date	Name	Date

CHAPTER 1

Designed, Not Default

The Theology of Fatherhood

> *"For this reason I bow my knees before the Father, from whom every family in heaven and on earth is named"*
>
> — Ephesians 3:14-15

Fatherhood is not a role you fell into — it is a calling you were built for. This chapter establishes the theological foundation of the entire study: God is Father first, and your fatherhood is meant to be a reflection of His. Most men are operating on default, shaped by the fathers they had or didn't have. This session asks you to name that pattern — and to begin choosing something different.

Chapter 1 also establishes why no man was designed to do this work alone — and what it means to both receive investment from other men and become that for someone else.

KEY VERSE

"For this reason I bow my knees before the Father, from whom every family in heaven and on earth is named"

— Ephesians 3:14-15

Write it out:

Chapter 1 argues it took five men to show the author the One — five because no one man could carry it all. Who are your five? If you cannot name five, who is one? And what does the gap mean?

What pattern did your father model for you — was he present but emotionally absent, completely absent, or genuinely engaged? Write it plainly: "The pattern I was handed is ________________" Now ask: am I repeating it, reversing it, or building something different?

When you operate on default — without intentionality, without deliberate effort — what does your fatherhood actually look like?

What does it mean to you that God is Father first — and that your fatherhood is meant to reflect His?

1. No man becomes who he was designed to be in isolation. Who are the men in your life right now who actually know where you are — not just what you do? Are you being known, or just seen?

2. What would it look like to be genuinely invested in another man's growth this year — not as a program, but as a relationship? What is stopping you from doing that right now?

3. Where is the gap between the father you default to and the father you were designed to be?

4. What does the phrase "God is Father first" actually change about how you see your role in your home?

ACCOUNTABILITY — 10 Minutes — This question is non-negotiable

What is one specific step you will take this week to be more intentional — not default — as a father? Name it specifically.

Name it specifically. Write it below. Read it to the group. Your facilitator will ask you about it next week.

Read Chapter 2 of *Built to Father* before the next session. As you read, identify which of the eight worldly pillars you have most defaulted to — and which SHEPHERD pillar feels most foreign to you right now.

CHAPTER 2

Two Fathers, Two Legacies

The Biblical Pillar vs. The Worldly Standard

> *"There is a way that seems right to a man, but its end is the way to death."*
>
> — Proverbs 14:12

Every man is building from one of two foundations: the worldly standard or the biblical one. The worldly standard is anchored to self — to achievement, appearance, and comfort. The biblical standard is anchored to God. This chapter introduces the full SHEPHERD framework and sets the eight worldly pillars against it. The question is not whether you are building — it is what you are building from.

KEY VERSE

"There is a way that seems right to a man, but its end is the way to death."

— Proverbs 14:12

Write it out:

Read the chapter. Then answer these questions privately before your group meets. Honest answers written before the group session make the conversation more real.

Marcus is the deliberate man — *the one who prays for his children by name, speaks identity into his daughter at the kitchen table, asks his wife on Friday how he did this week. Daniel is the man who has confused provision with presence, activity with intimacy — whose wife is lonely in a full house. Which one is closer to what your wife would say about you?*

Which of the eight SHEPHERD pillars is your strongest right now? Which is your weakest?

Where in your life do you use isolation — busyness, privacy, independence — as a hiding strategy?

Are you present in your home but emotionally checked out — there in body, absent in attention and intention? Or are you physically absent more than your family needs? Describe the pattern your children are actually experiencing, not the one you intend.

1. The chapter introduces the idea that worldly fatherhood is anchored to self and biblical fatherhood is anchored to God. Where do you feel that tension in your own life?

2. Which worldly pillar did your own father operate from? How has that shaped you?

3. The hiding question: if a man has no community, no accountability — is the honest answer that he hasn't found the right men, or that he doesn't want to be known?

4. What would it look like for your home to be built on the SHEPHERD framework rather than the worldly standard — starting this week?

<table><tr><td>ACCOUNTABILITY — 10 Minutes — This question is non-negotiable</td></tr><tr><td> </td></tr></table>

Pick the one SHEPHERD pillar that is most broken in your home right now. Name it to the group. What is one thing you will do this week to begin addressing it?

Name it specifically. Write it below. Read it to the group. Your facilitator will ask you about it next week.

Read Chapter 3 of *Built to Father*. Before the next session, spend five minutes on one Tuesday or Wednesday morning praying specifically for each person in your household by name. Notice what it reveals about where you are spiritually.

CHAPTER 3

Spiritual Leader

The Man Who Points His Family to God

"choose this day whom you will serve."

— Joshua 24:15

IN THIS SESSION

The S in SHEPHERD: Spiritual Leader. A man can attend church faithfully and still not be leading his family spiritually. Leading spiritually means your home has a direction — and you are the one holding the compass. This chapter confronts the gap between attendance and actual leadership, and calls men to take up a role most have quietly abdicated.

KEY VERSE

"Choose this day whom you will serve."

— Joshua 24:15

Write it out:

Are you leading your family spiritually — or attending church alongside them? What is the actual difference in your home on a Tuesday?

What does your personal prayer life look like? Do your children know you pray?

Where have you been passive in your spiritual leadership? Name a specific area.

What would it cost you — practically, daily — to take up the mantle of spiritual leadership in your home?

David — pastor, shepherd, one of the five men who shaped me — modeled spiritual leadership not in a classroom and not in a seminar, but in the everyday, mundane, glorious ordinariness of shared life. Meals. Late conversations. Accountability that had teeth. Who has modeled spiritual leadership for you in the ordinary?

Facilitator: choose 2–3 questions based on where the group is. You do not need to cover all of them. The accountability question at the end is non-negotiable.

1. What is the difference between being a spiritual leader and being a churchgoer? Which one are you?

2. What does your personal prayer life actually look like right now — not what you wish it looked like?

3. What would it look like to bring the Word into your home in one practical, sustainable way starting this week?

4. What fear or discomfort is keeping you from leading your family spiritually? Name it out loud.

ACCOUNTABILITY — 10 Minutes — This question is non-negotiable

Name one specific spiritual leadership practice you will begin or restore this week — not a resolution, an action. Praying at dinner, reading Scripture with your children, initiating a spiritual conversation. What is it, and when will you do it?

Name it specifically. Write it below. Read it to the group. Your facilitator will ask you about it next week.

BEFORE THE NEXT SESSION

Read Chapter 4 of *Built to Father*. Before the next session, initiate one spiritual conversation with your wife or a child — not a formal devotional, just a genuine moment. Note what it felt like to initiate.

CHAPTER 4

Husband Who Loves Sacrificially

The Man Who Loves Like Christ

"Husbands, love your wives, as Christ loved the church and gave himself up for her."

— Ephesians 5:25

Note for couples: This session is well-suited for husbands and wives to work through together. Consider doing the individual reflection questions separately, then discussing your answers with each other before or instead of bringing them to the group.

IN THIS SESSION

The first H in SHEPHERD: Husband Who Loves Sacrificially. Your marriage is either covenant or convenience — and the difference shows up not in the wedding vows but in the ordinary Tuesday. This chapter examines what it means to love your wife as Christ loved the church: not when she has earned it, not when it is easy, but as a deliberate, costly, unilateral commitment. The way you love your wife is the first thing your children learn about love.

"Husbands, love your wives, as Christ loved the church and gave himself up for her."

— Ephesians 5:25

Write it out:

INDIVIDUAL REFLECTION — Before the Group Meets

Read the chapter. Then answer these questions privately before your group meets. Honest answers written before the group session make the conversation more real.

Write your wife's obituary right now — two or three sentences. What does it say? What do you wish it said that it doesn't?

On a scale from covenant to convenience — where is your marriage operating right now? Be honest.

Where have you been loving your wife conditionally — with love that depends on her response, her mood, her effort? Name a specific pattern.

What is one covenant commitment you made to your wife that you have drifted from?

____

____

____

____

____

1. The chapter distinguishes between conditional love and covenant love. Which one is governing your marriage right now?

2. What is the hardest season your marriage has faced? What did it reveal about the foundation you were building on?

3. John Piper, in *This Momentary Marriage*, has argued that marriage is not primarily about your happiness — it is about displaying the covenant love of Christ for the church. Does your marriage display that? What would have to change for it to?

4. How does the state of your marriage affect your children? What are they learning about love and covenant from watching you and your wife?

5. What would it look like to love your wife this week in a way that costs

you something — not because she has earned it, but because of your commitment?

Name one specific way you will sacrificially love your wife this week — not a grand gesture, a deliberate, costly, specific act. Write it. Tell the group.

Name it specifically. Write it below. Read it to the group. Your facilitator will ask you about it next week.

BEFORE THE NEXT SESSION

Read Chapter 5 of *Built to Father*. This week, do one thing for your wife that she did not ask for, that costs you something, and that you do not mention afterward.

CHAPTER 5

Encourager & Nurturer

The Man Who Speaks Life

"Therefore encourage one another and build one another up, just as you are doing."

— *1 Thessalonians 5:11*

IN THIS SESSION

The first E in SHEPHERD: Encourager & Nurturer. There is a difference between praising what a child does and naming who a child is. Most men default to performance — good game, good grades, good job. But what a child carries for life is not the praise for what they did. It is the identity their father spoke over them. This chapter calls men to study their children and become fluent in the language of naming.

KEY VERSE

"Therefore encourage one another and build one another up, just as you are doing."

— *1 Thessalonians 5:11*

Write it out:

What specific identity did your father speak over you? If he was silent — what did his silence communicate?

When did you last speak something specific — not praise for performance, but named identity — over each of your children? What did you say?

What do you see in each of your children that you have not yet said out loud? Write it here.

Where do you nurture in your home — and where do you leave that work to your wife because it feels unnatural or uncomfortable?

1. The chapter talks about the difference between affirming performance and naming identity. What is the difference in practice?

2. What specific quality has God placed in each of your children that you have observed but perhaps not named?

3. What did it feel like — as a child — to either receive or not receive this kind of naming from your father? How has that shaped you?

4. What is one thing you can say to each of your children this week that speaks who they are, not just what they did?

Name each of your children. For each one, identify one specific quality God has placed in them. This week, you will speak that quality over them — by name, in the ordinary moment, not the ceremonial one. When and where will you do it?

Name it specifically. Write it below. Read it to the group. Your facilitator will ask you about it next week.

Read Chapter 6 of *Built to Father*. Before the next session, write down one specific quality you see in each of your children — not a performance, a characteristic. Bring what you wrote to the session.

CHAPTER 6

Protector & Provider

The Man Who Guards What He Loves

"He will cover you with his pinions, and under his wings you will find refuge; his faithfulness is a shield and buckler."

— Psalm 91:4

IN THIS SESSION

The P in SHEPHERD: Protector & Provider. Protection is not primarily about physical safety — it is about vigilance across five dimensions: spiritual, emotional, educational, physical, and digital. Most men are guarding the door but leaving the windows open. This chapter asks whether your wife is at peace — truly at peace — or whether she is carrying an alertness and vigilance that was never designed to be hers. Protection has a twin. Provision is stewardship — not just the paycheck, but the time invested in being ready, the money spent on what keeps your family safe, the discipline of staying current on the threats they face. A father who provides only financially has stewarded only part of what God entrusted to him. This chapter sits with both.

"He will cover you with his pinions, and under his wings you will find refuge; his faithfulness is a shield and buckler."

— Psalm 91:4

Write it out:

INDIVIDUAL REFLECTION — Before the Group Meets

Read the chapter. Then answer these questions privately before your group meets. Honest answers written before the group session make the conversation more real.

Where are you on the Cooper Color Code right now — white (unaware), yellow (alert), orange (threat identified), or red (reactive)? Be honest.

Which of the five dimensions of protection — spiritual, emotional, educational, physical, digital — is your weakest right now?

Is your wife at peace? Or is she carrying an alertness and vigilance that was never designed to be hers?

What is currently entering your home — digitally, relationally, spiritually — that you have not adequately guarded against?

Provision is stewardship. Where is your provision strong — and where is it costing your family in places money cannot reach? Are you providing the time it takes to stay ready? The attention it takes to see what is shifting in your home? The discipline it takes to walk the fence line in the quiet season? Name the gap between what you provide financially and what you provide otherwise.

1. The chapter expands protection far beyond physical safety. Which dimension of protection do you most tend to neglect?

2. What would it look like to be in yellow — appropriately alert — in your own home, with your own children?

3. How is your digital protection of your children? Do you know what they are seeing, who they are talking to, what is shaping them online?

4. Where is your wife carrying a burden of vigilance that should belong to you? What would it mean to take it back?

Name one specific protection gap in your home — spiritual, emotional, educational, physical, or digital. What is one concrete step you will take this week to address it?

Name it specifically. Write it below. Read it to the group. Your facilitator will ask you about it next week.

BEFORE THE NEXT SESSION

Read Chapter 7 of *Built to Father*. Before the next session, do an honest audit of one protection dimension in your home — particularly digital. Know what your children are seeing and who they are talking to.

CHAPTER 7

Heart of Integrity

The Man Who Is the Same in the Dark

> *"A man without self-control is like a city broken into and left without walls."*

> — Proverbs 25:28

IN THIS SESSION

The second H in SHEPHERD: Heart of Integrity. Integrity is not what you do when people are watching — it is what you do when no one is. The gap between the public man and the private man is the single most corrosive force in a family. Your children are learning what it means to be a person of character by watching you when you think they are not watching. This chapter calls men to close the gap.

KEY VERSE

"A man without self-control is like a city broken into and left without walls."

— Proverbs 25:28

Write it out:

Who are you when no one important is watching? Write the honest answer — not the version you are comfortable with.

The author was demoted before deployment — stripped of a team lead position he had earned — because of how he treated the men beneath him. When was the last time something you had earned was taken away because of who you had become? If the answer is never, is that because it hasn't happened yet, or because no one around you has been willing to tell you the truth?

Where is there a gap between your public face and your private conduct?
Name it specifically.

How do you treat the people who cannot help you — the server, the
cashier, the person beneath you at work?

What is the one area of your private life that, if your children knew about
it, would cost you something significant?

1. The key word in this chapter is *trust* — the currency of every relationship in your home. How is the trust account in your marriage right now? In your relationship with each of your children?

2. Where have you chosen comfort over integrity — the small compromise, the half-truth, the private habit?

3. The chapter talks about the gap between the public and private man. How wide is that gap in your life right now?

4. What would it take for your private life and your public life to be the same man?

Name one area where your private conduct does not match your public commitments. What is one specific step toward closing that gap this week?

BEFORE THE NEXT SESSION

Read Chapter 8 of *Built to Father*. Before the next session, identify one
area where your private conduct does not yet match your public
commitments. You do not need to share it with the group — but you
need to name it to yourself.

CHAPTER 8

Example Who Inspires Potential

The Man Who Calls Forth Destiny

"For we are his workmanship, created in Christ Jesus for good works, which God prepared beforehand, that we should walk in them."

— Ephesians 2:10

IN THIS SESSION

The second E in SHEPHERD: Example Who Inspires Potential. There is a version of fatherhood that is physically present and emotionally nowhere. Children who grow up in that house know what it feels like to be unseen. This chapter is about the father who studies his child the way God studied Gideon who names what God placed there before the fear arrived, before the evidence supports it, before the world has had its chance to say otherwise. The ceiling you live under is not the ceiling your children have to live under.

KEY VERSE

"For we are his workmanship, created in Christ Jesus for good works, which God prepared beforehand, that we should walk in them."

— Ephesians 2:10

Write it out:

Read the chapter. Then answer these questions privately before your group meets. Honest answers written before the group session make the conversation more real.

What was the presence pattern in your home growing up — was your father present and engaged, present but emotionally absent, or completely gone? Write it plainly. Now name the pattern you are currently handing to your own children.

What does it feel like to grow up in a home where someone is there but no one is watching? If you experienced this — how has it shaped you?

What is one "first" in your family that you have achieved? What ceiling did that raise for your children?

When you look at each of your children — what do you see in them that you have not yet named out loud?

GROUP DISCUSSION — 25 Minutes

Facilitator: choose 2–3 questions based on where the group is. You do not need to cover all of them. The accountability question at the end is non-negotiable.

1. The chapter distinguishes between inspiring potential and projecting

ambition. Which one are you doing with your children right now?

2. The angel of the LORD found Gideon hiding in a winepress and called him "mighty man of valor" — naming what God had placed in him before any evidence had surfaced. What does it look like for you to call your child "mighty man of valor" while they are still hiding? What would you actually say, to which child, this week?

3. What is the honest picture of your presence in your home right now — not what you intend, but what your children and your wife are actually experiencing? Are you present and engaged, present but absent, or somewhere in between? Are you breaking the presence pattern you inherited, or repeating it under a different name?

4. What would it look like for you to study your child this week — not evaluate their performance, but understand their nature?

ACCOUNTABILITY — 10 Minutes — This question is non-negotiable

Identify one specific quality God has placed in one of your children that you have not yet named. This week, you will look them in the eye in an ordinary moment and name it. Write what you will say.

Name it specifically. Write it below. Read it to the group. Your facilitator will ask you about it next week.

BEFORE THE NEXT SESSION

Read Chapter 9 of *Built to Father*. Before the next session, sit with one of your children for 15 minutes — not to evaluate their performance, but to observe them. What do you notice about who they are?

CHAPTER 9

Reprover & Wise Mentor

The Man Who Tells the Truth in Love

> *"By wisdom a house is built, and by understanding it is established."*
>
> — Proverbs 24:3

The R in SHEPHERD: Reprover & Wise Mentor. Most men default to one of two failure modes: they never say the hard thing, or they say it without love. Biblical reproof is different — it comes from relationship, it is specific, and it is offered in a spirit of gentleness. This chapter examines what it means to be the kind of man whose hard words land because the relationship underneath them is strong enough to hold them.

KEY VERSE

"By wisdom a house is built, and by understanding it is established."

— Proverbs 24:3

Write it out:

Read the chapter. Then answer these questions privately before your group meets. Honest answers written before the group session make the conversation more real.

Who in your life has earned the right to speak hard truth to you? Who have you given that access to?

Is there someone in your life — your wife, a child, a friend, a man you mentor — who needs to hear something from you that you have not yet said? What is stopping you?

What is the difference between reproof and criticism in your own experience of receiving both?

Where have you been passive — staying quiet when you should have spoken — to avoid conflict or discomfort?

1. The chapter describes a reproof from one of the author's mentors — seven words: "Since when has she stopped being God's daughter?" What made that reproof land? What made it possible?

2. Who are you? The passive bystander who never says the hard thing —
or the crushing critic who says it without love? Or somewhere on the
spectrum between them?

3. What does it mean to restore gently (Galatians 6:1) — to reprove
someone in a spirit of gentleness while keeping watch on yourself?

4. Is there a man in this room who needs to hear something from you that
you have been holding back? This is the place to say it.

ACCOUNTABILITY — 10 Minutes — This question is non-negotiable

Name one person in your life who needs to hear something true from you
this week. What is it? When will you say it? How will you say it in a spirit
of gentleness?

*Name it specifically. Write it below. Read it to the group. Your facilitator
will ask you about it next week.*

____

____

____

____

Read Chapter 10 of *Built to Father*. Before the next session, identify one person in your life — your wife, a child, a friend — who needs to hear something true from you. Prepare what you will say and how you will say it.

CHAPTER 10

Discipliner

The Man Who Loves Enough to Hold the Line

"For the LORD *disciplines the one he loves, and chastises every son whom he receives."*

— Hebrews 12:6

IN THIS SESSION

The D in SHEPHERD: Discipliner. Permissive parenting is not kindness — it is a form of neglect. A father who will not hold the line is a father who has chosen his own comfort over his child's formation. This chapter argues that loving discipline — consistent, calm, and rooted in the child's good rather than the father's frustration — is one of the most profound acts of love a man can offer his children.

KEY VERSE

"For the LORD *disciplines the one he loves, and chastises every son whom he receives."*

— Hebrews 12:6

Write it out:

Are you and your wife on the same page about discipline in your home? What would she say if asked?

Do you discipline in anger? Be honest. What does correction look like when you are exhausted, frustrated, or at the end of your capacity?

Is there a line in your home that you have stopped holding because holding it is too exhausting? Name it.

Does each of your children know — in the moment of correction — that you are for them, not against them?

1. The chapter says permissive parenting is its own form of neglect. Do you agree? Where have you chosen your own comfort over your child's formation?

2. Are you and your wife unified in your discipline — or do your children know how to navigate the gap between you?

3. What does it look like to discipline from love rather than from anger? What is the difference in practice?

4. What line have you stopped holding? What has it cost your child?

Name one specific boundary, standard, or line in your home that you have stopped enforcing. This week, you will re-establish it — with your wife's alignment, from love, not from frustration. What is it? When will you address it?

Name it specifically. Write it below. Read it to the group. Your facilitator will ask you about it next week.

Read Chapter 11 of *Built to Father*. Before the next session, have a brief conversation with your wife about one standard or boundary in your home that needs to be re-established or unified. Do not wait for the group session to act on it.

CHAPTER 11

The Generational Reach

Your Fatherhood Outlives You

*"Know therefore that the L*ORD *your God is God, the faithful God who keeps covenant and steadfast love with those who love him and keep his commandments, to a thousand generations."*

— Deuteronomy 7:9

IN THIS SESSION

Your fatherhood does not end when your children leave home. It extends forward into grandchildren you have not yet met, into marriages not yet formed, into a legacy that is being built or broken right now by choices you make this week. This chapter calls men to think in generations — to see themselves not just as fathers of the children in their home, but as the first link in a chain that can run a thousand generations deep.

KEY VERSE

"Know therefore that the LORD your God is God, the faithful God who keeps covenant and steadfast love with those who love him and keep his commandments, to a thousand generations."

— Deuteronomy 7:9

Write it out:

The author tells the story of three smashed car windows at sixteen — the moment the game could have felt rigged and he could have quit. He didn't. What was your smashed-windows moment? What did you do with it — and what did that decision make possible for the generation behind you?

What was the generational pattern handed to you — what did the men before you build or fail to build in terms of presence, faith, and character? What generational pattern are you now creating for the generation after you?

What do you want your grandchildren to inherit from you that cannot be put in a will?

Who are you praying for generationally? Do you pray for your children's future spouses?

1. The chapter talks about the "firsts" — the first in the family to do something, the ceiling raised. What first have you achieved? What did it open up for the generation behind you?

2. What are you building right now — and how much of it will outlast you?

3. What generational pattern does your family need you to break — the pattern of absence, passivity, silence, or fracture — and what does breaking it actually require of you this week, not eventually?

4. If your grandchildren could describe the legacy you left — not the money, the career, the accomplishments — what would you want them to say?

ACCOUNTABILITY — 10 Minutes — This question is non-negotiable

Name one specific thing you are building right now that will matter in the next generation. What is one step you will take this week to build it more deliberately?

Name it specifically. Write it below. Read it to the group. Your facilitator will ask you about it next week.

BEFORE THE NEXT SESSION

Read Chapter 12 of *Built to Father*. The chapter contains a diagnostic section called *When the Framework Fractures*. Read it slowly. Note which scenario or combination described your home or the home you grew up in. Come prepared to answer the reflection questions honestly.

CHAPTER 12

When You Have Failed

The Father Who Needs a Father

"If we confess our sins, he is faithful and just to forgive us our sins and to cleanse us from all unrighteousness."

— 1 John 1:9

Note for couples: This session is well-suited for husbands and wives to work through together. Consider doing the individual reflection questions separately, then discussing your answers with each other before or instead of bringing them to the group.

BEFORE YOU BEGIN THIS SESSION

This chapter contains a section called When the Framework Fractures — a diagnostic map of what happens when SHEPHERD pillars fail not one at a time but in combination. It covers: two pillars falling together, three pillars falling together, all-but-one scenarios, and the building going empty through slow quiet attrition. Read that section carefully before answering the reflection questions. The reflection and discussion for this session engage it directly. The map is not designed to condemn. It is designed to locate. The honest reader will find himself in it.

Every man in this study has failed. The question is not whether — it is what you do with the failure. This chapter maps the compound fractures that happen when multiple SHEPHERD pillars fail at once, and it points toward the only exit: specific, direct confession followed by specific, direct change. Guilt paralyzes. Conviction moves. This session is designed to move men from one to the other.

KEY VERSE

"If we confess our sins, he is faithful and just to forgive us our sins and to cleanse us from all unrighteousness."

— 1 John 1:9

Write it out:

INDIVIDUAL REFLECTION — Before the Group Meets

Read the chapter. Then answer these questions privately before your group meets. Honest answers written before the group session make the conversation more real.

The chapter contains a diagnostic map of compound pillar failures — two falling together, three, all but one, the building going empty. Read it slowly. Which scenario described your home? Write it here: "The combination I recognized was ________."

The framework fractures section makes this point: when one pillar fails, the load transfers — to the other pillars, to your wife, to your children. Who in your home is currently carrying load that was supposed to be yours? Name them and name what they are carrying.

What is the failure you most wish you could take back? Have you confessed it to the person it affected?

What is the difference between guilt and conviction in your own experience? Guilt paralyzes. Conviction moves. Which one are you living in right now with respect to your failures as a father or husband?

1. The "When Two Pillars Fall" section describes five specific compound failures. Which pairing landed hardest for you — and why? Where do you see it operating in your home or in homes you grew up in?

2. The chapter describes the man who is "physically present and has withdrawn from every pillar — not through dramatic departure but through slow, quiet attrition, one commitment at a time." Is that man in the room? Has that man been in the room at some point in the last year? This is the question worth sitting in.

3. The chapter talks about specific, direct confession: "I was wrong. Will you forgive me?" Not the general apology — the specific one. When did

you last do this with your wife? With each of your children?

4. The framework fractures map asks: "Which combination is the one you recognized? Which paragraph described your home?" The most important thing this chapter can do is move a man from reading the map to using it. What did you find on yours?

ACCOUNTABILITY — 10 Minutes — This question is non-negotiable

Name one specific failure — toward your wife or one of your children — that you have not fully owned. This week you will go to that person and say the specific words: I was wrong. Will you forgive me? Write what you will say.

Name it specifically. Write it below. Read it to the group. Your facilitator will ask you about it next week.

Read Chapter 13 of *Built to Father*. Before the final session, return to your accountability commitments from every previous week. Review what you wrote. Note where you followed through and where you did not. Come ready to give an honest account.

CHAPTER 13

Rise

The Man the World Is Waiting For

"Be watchful, stand firm in the faith, act like men, be strong. Let all that you do be done in love."

— 1 Corinthians 16:13-14

Note for couples: This is the closing session. Walk through it with your wife. The commitment you make here is not first a commitment to the group — it is a commitment to her. Read your final accountability answer to her before you read it to the room. The man who rises rises with his wife, not past her.

This is the final session. The question this chapter asks is not "what did you learn?" — it is "who are you now?" The world is not waiting for a perfect father. It is waiting for a man who knows what he was built for and is willing to rise to it — not eventually, not when the conditions are better, but now. This session is a commission, not a conclusion.

KEY VERSE

"Be watchful, stand firm in the faith, act like men, be strong. Let all that you do be done in love."

— 1 Corinthians 16:13-14

Write it out:

Why did you get married? Not the answer you give at dinner parties — the real one.

Why did you have children? Was it intentional, circumstantial, or a genuine calling?

Why do you continue to work? Is it provision, identity, or the debt that drives the overwork that drives the absence?

What is the one thing this book and this study have asked you to change that you have not yet changed? Name it. Write it down.

Facilitator: choose 2–3 questions based on where the group is. You do not need to cover all of them. The accountability question at the end is non-negotiable.

1. You have just spent thirteen weeks being formed. The book ends with "you are someone's five men — now, not later." Name him. First name, last name if you know it. What is the first step you will take toward him this month?

2. What is the one pillar this study has revealed as most broken in your home? What has changed — or what needs to change — in how you are approaching it?

3. The final word of *Built to Father* is: your legacy matters. What does your legacy look like right now — and what does it need to look like?

4. What kind of man does this group need you to be for them after these thirteen weeks are over? What does it look like to stay in each other's lives?

ACCOUNTABILITY — 10 Minutes — This question is non-negotiable

This is the final accountability commitment of the thirteen-week study. Name the one thing you are taking from this book that you will carry into the next year of your life. Not a vague intention — a specific commitment.

Write it. Ask them to hold you to it.

Name it specifically. Write it below. Read it to the group. This is the commitment you carry out of this room.

You are not the same man who opened this book.

You are an already there but not yet father. That is enough. That is the whole point.

YOUR LEGACY MATTERS.

"The righteous who walks in his integrity — blessed are his children after him!"

— Proverbs 20:7

What's Next

The thirteen weeks are over. The work is not.

What I have learned in years of working with men is that the group — if it was real — did something that is hard to replicate on your own. You were seen. You were held accountable. You were in a room with men who were trying to become something better than what they inherited. Do not let that end.

Here is what I would encourage you to do next. First, stay together. The group does not need a curriculum to meet. It needs men who are willing to keep showing up. A monthly breakfast, a standing check-in, a shared accountability text thread — any structure that keeps the commitments alive is worth building.

Second, start another group. The man who has been through this material is the most qualified person to lead another group through it. You do not need to have it figured out. You need to have been honest. If that is you, find four to eight men who need this and invite them in.

Third, give the book to someone. *Built to Father* exists because fatherlessness is not a private crisis — it is a generational one. Every man you hand this book to is a potential link in a chain that runs further than either of you can see.

The world is not waiting for a perfect father. It is waiting for a man who knows what he was built for and refuses to stop becoming it.

END OF THE STUDY GUIDE

About the Author

Doug Androsky is the founder and president of Fathering the Fatherless, a nonprofit organization built around a single conviction: that a father's legacy is not measured by what he achieves but by what he passes on.

Doug's work begins with a recognition that most men were never shown what fatherhood fully looks like — not because their fathers did not love them, but because their fathers were working from incomplete frameworks themselves. The SHEPHERD model emerged from years of study, counseling, and his own reckoning with what it means to be the kind of father a family is designed to need.

He is the author of *Built to Father*, the foundational volume in the series; *When the Framework Fractures*, the diagnostic companion that maps all 247 failure combinations across the SHEPHERD framework; and *Built to Father: The Study Guide*, the application workbook you are holding. All three books orbit the same conviction: that a man who understands what he is carrying — and what it is costing — is a man who can choose to change it.

Fathering the Fatherless operates on the conviction that intentional fatherhood — pursued honestly and rebuilt when it fractures — changes families across generations. The work is not theoretical. It is personal.

Fathering the Fatherless
fatheringthefatherless.org

Also in the Built to Father Series

Book One

Built to Father

The SHEPHERD Framework for Fathers

The foundational volume. Introduces all eight pillars of the SHEPHERD framework and builds the complete architecture of intentional fatherhood — what each pillar means, why it matters, and what it costs a family when it is missing. The primary text that this Study Guide is designed to apply.

Book Two

When the Framework Fractures

The Complete Diagnostic Companion to Built to Father

The diagnostic companion. Maps all 247 failure combinations across the SHEPHERD framework — from two pillars failing simultaneously to seven failing while one remains. If you are working through this Study Guide and finding that specific pillars are carrying more damage than a session can address, *When the Framework Fractures* names exactly what that combination is costing your family and what it looks like from the inside.

Appendix A: The SHEPHERD Framework

Built to Father is built around eight pillars of biblical fatherhood. Every session in this guide engages one or more of these pillars. Keep this page in mind as you work through the study.

S	**Spiritual Leader**	*The man who points his family to God. He leads from his knees. His home has a spiritual direction because he is the one holding the compass.*
H	**Husband Who Loves Sacrificially**	*The man who loves like Christ loved the church — not conditionally, not conveniently, but covenantally. His love costs him something.*
E	**Encourager & Nurturer**	*The man who speaks life. He names identity, not just performance. His words land in his children's bones and stay there.*
P	**Protector & Provider**	*The man who guards what he loves — spiritually, emotionally, digitally, physically. His family is at peace because he is on watch.*
H	**Heart of Integrity**	*The man who is the same in the dark. His private life matches his public life. His children are learning what a man of character looks like.*
E	**Example Who Inspires Potential**	*The man who calls forth destiny. He studies his children, names what God placed in them, and becomes a ceiling-raiser for the next generation.*
R	**Reprover & Wise Mentor**	*The man who tells the truth in love. He speaks hard things gently. He mentors not just his children but the men around him.*
D	**Discipliner**	*The man who loves enough to hold the line. His discipline comes from love, not frustration. His children know he is for them, not against them.*

Each of the 13 sessions in this guide focuses on one or more of these pillars. The Discipliner pillar (D) is covered in Chapter 10. The full framework is introduced in Chapters 1 and 2.

Appendix B: Facilitator Guide & Session Format

The facilitator of a *Built to Father* group does not need to be a therapist, a pastor, or a man who has this figured out. He needs to be three things: honest, present, and unwilling to let the group stay comfortable when comfortable means shallow.

The following notes are not optional reading. They are the operating instructions for a group that actually changes men.

Your Role

You are not teaching this material. *Built to Father* does that. Your role is to create the conditions in which men can be honest — and then to hold the space when they are. That means you ask more than you speak. It means you share your own honest answer before you ask anyone else to share theirs. It means you do not rescue men from silence, because silence in a room full of men who are actually thinking is one of the most productive things that can happen in a session.

Before Each Session

Read the chapter the group will be discussing. Answer the individual reflection questions yourself — in writing, privately, before the meeting. Choose 2–3 discussion questions that feel most alive for where your group is right now. Pray specifically for each man by name. Know which man in the room is likely to need the most space this week and which man is likely to fill the space with noise to avoid being seen.

Managing the Room

Some men will talk to avoid vulnerability. They give long, articulate, theologically correct answers that communicate nothing about where

they actually are. Your job is to notice this and ask the follow-up question
that interrupts it: That is a good answer — but where are you with this
personally, right now, in your own home?

Some men will go silent because they are carrying something heavy and
do not know if the room is safe enough to say it. Your job is to make the
room safe by going first. Every session, share one thing that is genuinely
hard for you. Not a testimony — a live, current struggle. Men follow what
they are shown.

If a man in the group discloses something that indicates a crisis — a failing
marriage, an addiction, a situation involving serious harm to himself or
others — do not treat the group setting as the appropriate container for
that disclosure. Follow up with him privately after the session. Know the
names of two counselors or pastors you can refer him to before the group
ever starts.

The Accountability Question

This is the most important ten minutes of every session. Every man
names one specific thing he will do differently this week. Not a general
intention — a specific action. "I will apologize to my son for the way I
spoke to him on Thursday" is an accountability commitment. "I will try to
be more patient" is not.

The following week, before moving into the new chapter, return to last
week's accountability commitments. Ask each man to report — not to
perform, but to be honest. What happened? What got in the way? What
did you learn? A group that does not follow up on accountability
commitments is a group that is having interesting conversations rather
than becoming different men.

Pace and Format

The recommended session length is 55 minutes. Shorter than this and the accountability question gets cut. Longer than this and the group loses energy. Thirteen chapters over thirteen weeks is the standard format. Some groups choose to add a fourteenth session specifically for the group covenant, held before Chapter 1 begins.

The group works best at 4–8 men. Fewer than four and there is not enough diversity of experience in the room. More than eight and the accountability question becomes a performance for an audience rather than a commitment to brothers.

A Note on the Wound Sections

Each chapter of *Built to Father* contains a Wound section — a direct, unflinching description of what it costs a child, a wife, and a marriage when a pillar is absent. These sections will surface pain in your group. Men who grew up without fathers, men who have already done damage they cannot undo, men who recognize themselves in the wound description — these men will need the room to be safe when the chapter's wound hits them. Do not move past the wound too quickly. It is doing necessary work.

A Note on Thematic Overlap

Chapter 5 and 8 share a related theme — speaking identity into children — but approach it from different angles: Chapter 5 focuses on the words a father speaks, Chapter 8 on the presence and vision behind them. If your group notices the overlap, name it directly: that's not repetition, that's the framework doing its work.

Appendix C: The Session Format

Every session follows the same structure. The format is a container — the conversations will be different each week, but the container stays consistent. Men know what to expect. That consistency is itself a form of trust.

Opening Check-In — 5 minutes
One word. That is all. Each man says one word that describes where he is this week — not a sentence, not an explanation, just one word. This is not small talk. It is a temperature read. The facilitator pays attention to which words are heavy and which men could not land on just one word because there is too much underneath it.

Accountability Follow-Up — 10 minutes
Return to last week's accountability commitments. Each man reports honestly: What happened? What did you do? What got in the way? The facilitator does not shame the man who failed. He asks what the failure revealed. The man who succeeded gets acknowledged — and then asked what it cost him to follow through.

Reading Review — 5 minutes
Open questions: What stood out from this chapter? What did you want to skip past? What challenged you? What was one thing you highlighted or could not stop thinking about after you finished reading? This is not a comprehension check. It is an invitation to the part of the material that is already alive for each man.

Group Discussion — 25 minutes
The facilitator has chosen 2–3 questions from this guide. He opens with his own honest answer. Then he invites the group. He is watching for the men who are performing versus the men who are present. He is not afraid

of silence. He is not in a hurry to fill it.

Accountability Commitment — 10 minutes

Every man names one specific action he will take before the next session. Not a resolution — an action. Specific, observable, and tied directly to what was covered in this chapter. He writes it in the space provided. He reads it to the group. The group acknowledges it. The facilitator writes it down.

Prayer — 5 minutes

The facilitator or a designated man prays for the group — each man by name, for his wife, for his children. Not a formulaic closing prayer. A specific, personal intercession for the men in the room and for what they are carrying home.

Total session time: 55 minutes. If your group runs long on discussion, the accountability commitment is the last thing you cut, not the first. A session that ends without an accountability commitment has produced a good conversation. A session that ends with every man having named a specific action has produced a different man.

www.ingramcontent.com/pod-product-compliance
Lightning Source LLC
Chambersburg PA
CBHW040908130726
48005CB00019BA/3023